Do Songbirds Know Where They're Singing

Do Songbirds Know
Where They're Singing

John B. Lee

First Edition

Wet Ink Books
www.WetInkBooks.com
WetInkBooks@gmail.com

Do Songbirds Know Where They're Singing
by John B. Lee

Cover Image – John B. Lee
Cover Image Detail – Price of Peace Monument in Ortona, Italy
Cover Design – Richard M. Grove
Layout and Design – Richard M. Grove

Typeset in Calibri Light
Printed and bound in Canada
Distributed in USA by Ingram,
      – to set up an account – 1-800-937-0152

Library and Archives Canada Cataloguing in Publication

Title: Do songbirds know where they're singing / John B. Lee.
Other titles: Do songbirds know where they are singing
Names: Lee, John B., 1951- author.
Identifiers: Canadiana 20250259478 | ISBN 9781998324248 (softcover)
Subjects: LCGFT: Poetry.
Classification: LCC PS8573.E348 D6 2025 | DDC C811/.54—dc23

About The Price of Peace Monument

The Price of Peace Monument is located in the Piazza Plebiscito in Ortona, Italy. This powerful memorial was commissioned by a group of Canadian Veterans who had held a special reunion in 1998 in the town where they had fought during the Second World War. Designed by Canadian artist Rob Surette, it was unveiled in 1999 to commemorate the sacrifices and achievements of our soldiers during the Battle of Ortona.

During Christmas 1943, the historic town of Ortona along the Adriatic coast was the scene of vicious fighting in the Italian Campaign. Its steep, rubble-filled streets limited the use of tanks and artillery and made it an infantryman's battle. Over the course of several days of hard combat, the Canadians often smashed their way through walls and buildings—"mouseholing" as they called it – to avoid having to attack through the deadly streets that were swept by enemy fire. It would be some of the toughest fighting of the war for the Canadians and many of them became casualties before the town officially fell on December 28, 1943.

The square where the Price of Peace Monument is located was badly damaged and the base of the memorial incorporates bricks from buildings that had been smashed in the fighting. Atop the memorial is a bronze, life-sized sculpture of a wounded Canadian soldier being comforted by a comrade.

The cover photograph taken by the author shows a section of the Price of Peace Monument located in the Paizza Plebiscitio in Otrana Italy. In the photograph one can see the face of a fallen soldier being comforted by a medic.

This book is dedicated to the memory of my wife's father Ernest Otto Morden who fought with the Canadian Forces in the liberation of Italy from December 1943 until the summer of 1944, and for my paternal uncle John Crosby Lee who served in the Canadian Navy during the war including his having been on a ship sweeping the waters of the English Channel for mines on D Day in the wee hours of the morning on June 6, 1944.

"O race of men, how many storms and misfortunes must thou endure, and how many shipwrecks, because thou, beast of many heads, strugglest in many directions!"

Book One of
"De Monarchia"
Dante Alighieri

Table of Contents

Do the Songbirds Know They're Singing

Lest We Forget

A Shepherd's Duty
to the Lamb*

when I was a boy
it seemed more memory
to me of things remembered
than a reading
of things I'd never done
or known
as Caesar warred
against the Gauls
I thought, almost I thought
I had been there
with short sword and shield
in plumed helmet, my body
breasted in leather
my feet in sandals ankle laced
with greaves
like tree bark round my shins
and cutting through
the thronging flesh of men
like scything nettles
in the fencerows on the farm
oh, I felt in reading
those battle words
that I'd been there as one
among the centurions
in the legions of Rome
one golden hour at the death of day
the crimson sun a slash at heaven's rim
cutthroat horizons hot
as hematomas at the edge of fallen time

and so
in a tourist bus
we crossed and crossed again
the river Caesar crossed
we crossed with ease of weaving on a loom

the Rubicon of soldiers
on the way to Rome
and we were adult tourists
of more recent wars

to think of greatness
weeping at the sorrow
of another tyrant's youth
the disappointed warrior
with a general's hubris

and was I ever
young enough
to think myself
a hero's ghost
within a callow frame
oh foolish boy
be grateful in your bones
for the gentler and general ennui
that comes with peace
and know that ancient victors
fall to this more valiant truth

the meadows of Elysium
are meant to feed the lambs
and you've a shepherd's duty
even to the lion's shadow on a soldier's grave

*When I was a boy reading Caesar's conquests I wondered if I
weren't a reincarnation of a soldier from that time, it seemed so
familiar to me in my youth and a month ago in May in visiting
Italy as part of a tour of the battlefields of WWII, we crossed the
Rubicon several times on our tour bus.

Do the Songbirds Know
They're Singing

Dear Ola

My wife Cathy and I toured the battle sites of WWII in Italy. One of the first graveyards we visited in Sicily was alive with sunlight, shade, and birdsong. The only reminder of the sacrifices of war were the graves of fallen Canadians. Almost everywhere we went, we were honoured as descendants of soldiers who fought and who lost their lives in the war in Italy fighting against the Germans in the towns and villages and in the countryside and now peaceful river valleys of Sicily and the Italian mainland. I wondered as I stood by the grave markers of the fallen Canadians, many as young as 17, 18, and 19, as I stood in the sound of birds singing, I thought of this title for a series I hoped to write, Do the Songbirds Know Where They're Singing, and a phrase spoken by an officer after the great sacrifice of battle, "They were fine boys, all of them gone, all gone ..." This heartfelt tribute to the young who lost their lives in their late teens and early twenties, a time when I was in high school, and in early years of university, and I felt the loss deeply.

A person on the tour asked me, knowing that I was a poet, if I could sum up my feelings about the tour in a single word. I thought of the word "loss", not a joyful word, though being young, there was much joy and jubilation as an antidote to the noise and chaos and cordite and blood-in- the-soil stink of war. I thought the word "loss" as in loss of life, loss of youth, loss of innocence, loss of peaceful dreaming, even upon returning home, the cocoon of silence woven around the horrors of war, the memories buried so deep in the mind that the psyche could not handle remembering, except the memory of moments of celebration, youthful hijinks, and the ironic treatment they had for being called "the D Day Dodgers," by an English parliamentarian, the song they sang ending "If you look around the mountains and through the mud and rain/ You'll see the rows of crosses, some which bear no name/ Heartbreak and toils and suffering gone/ The boys beneath, they linger on/ They were some of the D Day Dodgers/ And they're still in Italy."

The struggle to liberate Italy from Fascists and the occupying forces of Germany resulted in the deaths of nearly 6,000 Canadians and slightly more Germans. That's one million dead in a few months from their arrival in Sicily, and their entry into the Italian boot from the south, and their fighting their way in winter rains, and summer heat, from early 1943 until late summer 1944. My father-in-law, Ernest Otto Morden was a sergeant who fought at Ortona, and the Liri River Valley, then again at the Gothic line, until going from there to France and finally into Germany.

Dear Ola, I tell you these things because I know you suffer from the terrible news coming out of Ukraine, as we also suffer for the Jewish soldiers and civilians and the Arab citizens of the Gaza strip. War is always a failure of the human imagination. Even WWII, is traceable to the peace of November 1918 when war reparations were imposed on Germany which were greater than the GNP of planet earth. Little wonder that we should reap the whirlwind when we are so poorly served by our governments.

When Churchill was asked, "What shall we call this conflict that engages us?", he is said to have replied, "The unnecessary War." He said this having warned his own government and the governments of the western world of the military buildup in Germany, and the slow-moving seizure of power by Adolf Hitler.

A Jewish scholar was asked, "How shall we ever come to understand the horrors of the Holocaust?" He is said to have replied, "Even an effort to understand such evil is a sin. The desire to understand it means you accept that it is within human understanding, and therefore, it is embraced by comprehension. No! It is beyond human understanding. It is outside of the realm of humanity. We dare not think to comprehend it, lest by understanding we come to embrace it. It is a sin to even attempt to understand it."

That is a fascinating insight into human comprehension of pure evil. It destroys the very one who would. contain it in the mind. Like a doomed Hobbit wearing Gollum's ring, we retch and puke and vomit and belch the name of 'evil' Gollum Gollum Gollum. Like the German commandant at the end of the film The Zone of Interest, dry heaving in his uniform as he strides the otherwise empty halls, in his jackboots, he bends over twice, and dry heaves, unable to throw up what his body and mind have consumed by his participation in the evil in which he was a major participant. An enthusiastic and coldly passionate Nazi, he knew deep down inside that he was digging a black abyss where his soul had once flickered as a little flame in youth. He had extinguished that flame, and he had allowed his dispassionate hatred for himself and for humanity to drop down in darkness, a darkness visible.

I once wrote a poem with the question, "What happens to the darkness when you fill the vase?" Even the purest and clearest and most limpid waters will not displace the darkness. You must carry a light where you go. And if you have snuffed that candle, you drop down and down and down in ever deeper darkness with no light to show you how clear the waters of the well within the body.

*This is an email I sent to my friend.
the poet Ola Nowosad
whose family are of Ukrainian heritage.

The Songbirds
of Auschwitz

what are they singing
the songbirds of Auschwitz
and what of the bees
in the roses of ash
beneath a blue sky
which is cloudless and grey
and brilliant with light
in the morning like embers
come over the wall

and what of the night
with its lovely velarium of stars
where Draco
and Beetlejuice shine
among monsters we might trace with our eyes
as we chart there the rumours of God

I think of the moment
one man in his ship
who orbits the moon
as he enters the darkness
alone where no one has gone
into the blackness of space
as deep as a cave
like the heart in his breast
or the soul in his flesh
or the cut of a whip in the wind

Moths in the Bergamot

... for John Keats

at first sight
in the weed-thick greenery
the bee balm
stands tall
leaping out at the light
in ragged lavender and rent pink
blooms tattering the untended field
in seemingly shredded petals
like the tossing out
of discarded coat buttons
landing in tatterdemalion
dozens as though
worn threadbare by thumbs
of a busy seamstress
goddess of silver needles in need of
new material
stop here reader —
pause on these words
linger in each syllable
become the moth's hunger for detail
as with your pinwheel tongue
unfurling you lick
the difficulty presented
by the minty fragrance
of the nearly purple lances
thrusting at blue heaven
as heaven is also rooted
in earth
where roots seek water
and hold to a liquid fascination
as a mind might come clear
to the truth

and then upon taking
a closer look
as though with a winged proboscis
that blunted sentient thread
of the swallowtail and
the weird imago
of the hummingbird moth
each in slow discovery
finding how the flower longs
to yield the deep secrets
of the poet's soul
withheld from most ...

the busy child inside the old man
is swatting the meadow
with a torn net
he sees himself as a young warrior
decapitating the quick-to-die grasses
catching nothing but wind
in motion and motion of wind
and the dream-seed possibility
when the old man
stays his arm
and says   look

Do the Songbirds Know
Where They're Singing

a poem composed in Agira Canadian War Cemetery
on a beautiful morning in May

the clouds like Valkyries
cast their unreadable shade
in the shadows of this light-receiving green
while the songbirds
sing in glorious celebration
of the life within
the full-throated arias
of May
which is primavera
to the halcyon hallelujahs
of this sacred day
they seem to be praying
in song
from deep within
the soft-leafed branches
where the breeze
is a full-breathed
reminder of the sighing
of a sacred sycamore
having its quiet say
and do they know anything
of the sheltered sorrows
of the war dead
sleeping there
like children in the quilted counterpane
of a bedroom stolen safe away
in endless mornings
of their lost youth
where they remain
as reverential dreamers do
under the stylized stones
that bear their stolen names
as though they were writ upon a chiseled list

oh, how I wish
as these songbirds seem to do
in the euphonious beauty
of their whistling on
as though of an unequal peace
that we might know nothing
of the loss
not by a strange indifference
but rather
by an innocent gathering up
of each life unlived
with a given gift
of sixty candles more
for each
and a breath of wishes
to bend each flame within the breast
that's been stilled by the horrors of war

Bury Them Deep

"bury them deep, for the dogs are hungry" Instructions
from an officer to those assigned to burial details in Italy

bury them deep
for the dogs are hungry
and this then
is the ravenous
appetite of the dogs of war
that these dead boys
should be a meal
to the meaning of moonlight
that loves the water loss it shined upon
as the darkness
loves the grave that seeks
the deep reflection
of the waves of earth that pulse
upon these human shores
go measure time
the way a sleeper might
who pulls the counterpane
in dream
to warm the bones
of night
this is the voice of loam
this sorrow
in the soil
when blind awakening
the soul's like spittle on a candlewick
this smothering's a shovel's worth
to mask the face
that wears the mask of clay
then set a walker's burden there
a living green upon the sheltered heart

like cellar fruit are we
or cobwebbed wine
that sours in the dark
cold-framed in frost

these shallow dogs
that fan the scree
to rattle up
a lifeless hand
these sextants of the dead
make salutations
like a shaken glove
to give a second life its last farewell

... if we worry about love, why not war

imagine my uncle
his intended beloved
blown to a ghost
in the blitz
her body seeding the blasted streets
life lost in crimson rubble
her spirit rising like brick dust
smouldering up and out
from the ruination of a building's romance
suddenly deaf to the sound
of sirens
and the otherwise
forgotten horrors
of these deadly heavens
the Luftwaffe heartless
and heroic
like a locust storm
thick with lost angels
sawing the crop of a doomed generation
their bomb doors
shitting death on the city
and though she was a simple
flesh-and-blood woman
photographed in a nurse's rank
she surrendered herself
to the mournful memory of grieving

as it is
with each light
we take to the grave
that luminous fire still glowing in ash
those lips
like roses in gauze
that name
on a whispering stone
two hearts for the earth
one to bury
one to carry away

The Bellwether Grazing

Polish Cemetery, Italy

the bellwether
is grazing
near the graves of the dead from war
nipping the grass
with a gentle
tintinnabulation
as though
calling the flock
to partake in the sweet green
succulent and sacred grief
of heaven's reminder
that she
is the blue sister
to the earth
as the rain
that slakes the rising of the well
might also weave the woven roots
beneath the loam
an intermingling
of fragrant thirst
within the water-seeded wind
a gentle swath
that wets the wool
go follow then
this spirit path
with acres edged in woe
the living step to count their sleeps
since when
this storied day
went silent
as all our sorrows do
while what the shepherd hears
confounds the soul
as to the whereabouts
of sound

The Olive Trees of Ortona

the olive trees of Ortona
were coming into flower
forgetful of the wars we waged
some eighty Mays ago
with hard fruit
yet to form
as green things will
in time
when green time gives its heart
to youth in spring
with promissory vines
of autumn wine to drink away
in winters red with song

how reconcile
this peaceful earth
with battle smoke
and battle noise
and blasted ground
where bloodied men and boys not men
lie crushed about
and broken in the brain
so limbless they were but
a lessening of tailor's work
a smaller count of sleeves
each stranger
in a stranger's dream
came home to stolen sleeps

how like a barber's conversation
with a ghost
whose hair is silver in the glass
it is
to contemplate
this swindler's conjuring
of things unseen

the ass that turns the wheel
to grind
this virgin hour
of its oil
comes round and round
and round again
to show this harlequin and horse
that leap and fall like waves
upon a newly painted carousel

here grave eruptions
sooth the grass
with roses fragrant of the day

while buried men
stay buried
beneath a faith of stone

The Inquiry

when an officer inquired
as to why
the soldier in the heat of battle
lay flat to the earth
face down
full out, like the newly dead
he is said to have replied
"I'm looking
 for a goddamn four-leaf clover
 with my nose"

like a he goat nipping the grass
or a bison bull
grazing on deep-rooted
blue gamma come out of the earth
in the plains, grown tall even
in the absence of rain

why don't you
who would talk of war
in the speakeasy
war at a summer fête
war from an easy chair
in a warm parlour
all winter away from the storm
then try your own luck
at survival
in a kill zone
you in this zeitgeist
of the water fountain
talking big for the boss
as it is with too many
middle-age men
waxing eloquent
over the suffering of strangers

in that
knocked-flat argument
that should come
like a fire to the tongue
in words bitter as pipe spittle
and wet smoke

but these suggestions
of lazy-boy glory
come as hookah-cooled
almost mentholated
peppermint flavoured gum-chewers language
oh, wise dragon, oh risible worm

when Hitler said – be heartless
where were your ears
and when he praised Heydrich
as the man with an iron heart
did you listen
as a generation fell to the gleaner
like a wheat harvest
lain flat by fire and hail
with seed-useless as a dropped broom

so, go lie on the grass by a grave
and truffle
the ground
like a hog
if you think to find yourself
Sunday-school brave
in a braggart's bellicose mood
because you're all for
sending the young into battle
then say you believe in the rumble of thunder
and the scour of flame
as the wind-quivered
clover you seek
lops its green ear under
the shell-weight of snails
and shines as though with a wish to be found

Galileo's Observatory, Florence

... the German generals turned Galileo's telescope upon the enemy to make observations as to the whereabouts of their foe

not on the heavens trained
where Galileo proved
the earth was but a lowly satellite
in crushed rotation round
the sun
and so became a heretic
to Rome
whose inquisition feared
the simple science
of an uncomplicated glass
and so
they set a fire
burning in the mind of man
and kindled it with fear of truth
as immolation
is a coward's proof
of pusillanimous and mortal flesh
no Florentine
a-flower in flame
that blooms in darkness
cell by cell
could light the lifted eye
that snuffs the soul
recanted like the wine of smoke
that smudges skin
like blushing
from a thought recoiling to
that which mortifies what lies within
old Aristotle's shadow and Apollo's shade

float upon the fiery pages
that drift in thermals, up and up
like angels
in the attitude and altitude of self-deluding priests

here the temple falls again
and here
the Sadducees of war
turn telescopes
in general decline
to seek the presence
of a more recent foe
as we are also enemies
of sunlight
and her sister moon
come close
and closer still
the lens seduces light
and brilliant darkness
burns the distant hill
as antiquated stars
immortalize a second ignorance
far deeper than the first

Walking the Streets
of Florence

we were walking the streets
of Florence
when we were caught
in the rain
as were the statues of the city
we straggled
in the weather, suffering
the same downpour
that drenched each sculpted stone
as with a thought
for Dante Alighieri
locked away
sepulchral in Ravena on the Adriatic coast
where we'd also
strolled the sand that washed against
the waters of the sea
while Virgil
was a shadow close at hand

and we were there
to think upon
the wonders and the horrors
of the lifespan
since the world of war
when hell
scribed seven circles
round each solitary man
as in a womb
of fire
we are born

and on that tourist promenade
upon the ozone
fragrant streets of art
we felt the soak
of heaven's life
as present in the senses
of the living flesh

I tell you reader
I was there
and I felt the quitting
of the quickening wet
like the drying of the fabric
on a laundry line
with blood within my marrow bone
and spittle breath
within these words
like ink that glittered on the pages
of an empty tomb
or chisels
set aside when the stone is satisfied
to still the sculptor's moving hand

The Revenant

the rebuilding of the Benedictine monastery at Monte Cassino

At the time of the campaign to liberate Italy from Fascism and German occupation during the war, it had been agreed upon by the German high command and the allies that certain sites would be spared because of their architectural significance. The Benedictine monastery at Monte Cassino was one such location. The allies had agreed to spare the monastery, that is until it was (wrongly) rumoured to be occupied by German soldiers using the altitude of that location to spy upon the movement of British and Canadian troops. The decision was made to bomb the monastery into rubble, which they did. After the war the local Italians decided to rebuild the monastery to the exact specifications of the original structure. They accomplished this miracle of reconstruction in a little over a decade, giving priority to this project over the rebuilding of their own communities. The monastery now stands upon a hill overlooking the Liri valley, a majestic symbol of mankind's will to honour past glories.

three times a day
like burdened beasts
the women of the lower town
would walk
the winding path
to climb the hill
with stones
in service to the mason's hod
as puzzled workers
built the walls
that fell to bombs
and as it is
with architectural ants
in sandy pismires
kicked to dust
beneath a grateful sky
the shattered statues
rose again against
revivifying shadows
in the shape of broken saints
collapsing as they did
in flames
heretical to war

see how blue heavens
calm the earth
with labours of the hive
what's manufactured
in the comb
is also in the root
and in the stem
the flower drones
against the lion's fractured jaw
to make a weapon gripped
to draw
a bony circle where creation
kilns the fire
that shapes the brick

go burn the drafter's plats
we've nothing left to do
but this, and this again
and this ...

Walking Down
to the Melfa River
Eighty Years
after the War

the day we walked
down to the banks
of the Melfa River
in remembrance of the battle
at the crossing in the war
all the way down
the nearly broken way
I thought of cows
careful of the path
beset by random flops
like greasy landmines
the kind that smear
the shoes
in soft explosions
of crusted dung
breaking open to a green
and slimy ooze
where beetles buzz
and bottleflies huzzah

the farm beyond the fence
beside the broken road
where milk cows
clocked their tails
like filthy pendulums
or mantle metronomes
meant to measure music
lowing at the saw-jawed hay

as we arrived
where weed work swayed
against the breath-weight of the wind
as wading through
the greening gorse
some sought
the easy water's edge
becalmed beneath the shadow
of an overpass

here where Caesar might have stepped
or Visigoths
and Vandals wet their swords in gore
while others
dropped their shields in thirst
conquests of chaos
drumming like the hearts
of troubled ghosts
those dying fires seen through fog

meanwhile
the cows seem curious of us
of we who walking
peaceful pastures
felt the pastoral idylls
of this Eden here
as they licked their noses
clean of oats and corn

Crossing the River
on a Bridge of Skulls

it sometimes seems to me
that we are crossing the river
on a bridge of skulls
all those thought-filled bones
like stones in the shallows
this war of minds
and the river is the river of time
it is also the river of blood
and we've paid the ferryman
with green-faced coppers
the kind you find
in a what-not drawer
with old screws
and broken open locks
a skeleton key your grandfather used
on a strongbox
and the water is sorrowing
over the shallows of a lost graveyard
flooding the catacombs
and floating the bones
of a broken oak
can't you feel with your footfall
how the far side
is foxed with dangers
and you're the wraith of a rabbit
twitching your ears like an old tv
your whiskers, the ones you missed shaving
with the weakening eyes of an old man
needing a nurse to pinch your nose
and tip your head back
for the want of the razor she's wolfing

for the cutthroat moment
the way the moon turns red for women
and we sink to the hairline
as the next generation gone mad
with gulping and having our say
about drowning

Pax Romana

like the bullet holes
in the wooden clinkers
of the church at Batoche
those irreparable remnants of war
were evident everywhere
in the city of Rimini
and the hamlet of San Maria
those Italian towns
with the masonry still chipped by shells

these quiet reminders
like insects working a wall
the bruised brick
bored through as though by the straying of wasps
in soft fruit
burrowing in where ripeness weeps
from a sticky hole gone amber with
nectar from the rot of an orchard's summer desires

here in this quiet noise of recent May
this silent and shrapnel-shaped day
worried with wonder
where the tanks once
wandered as slow beasts in armour
primordial with the rumble of fire
like the walking of dragons
dragging their spiked tails
and lashing the rubble of streets in ruin

there we were
in the long lacuna of a formidable blue
as though the storming were only recently over
and life-taking thunder
had never forked through with lightning
licking the wind slashing and rending
the billowing silk of new heavens

when death in the shocked light
and death in the electrified darkness
came as a cut-line of flame

not since Caesar, not
since the Goths not since
the Visigoths and Vandals
has the scab-scarred vanity of Man
healed over such historical truths ...

we are all of us
mad in the heart
and wild in the mind
leaving love wailing in a cradle
though it thirsts in its soul for a dead breast gone dry

Roma Puo Aspettore*

there is an ever-present thought of war
burning in the mind of man
imagine the ghost of Il Duce
punching the air
on a balcony in Rome
overlooking an adoring crowd
his fist clenched
his jaw set
in an all-too-familiar bone-locked face
the ever-revenant bellicosity
of the scowling tyrant
whose heart drops and rises
like hard fruit
that clings to the shadow cage
of high branches
when storm winds shake
a flickering chiaroscuro of temporal darkness

I think of this as I stand
a tourist in these streets
of the eternal city
looking up at where
he once stood
in his military costume
a tailor's jest
surely, a milliner's joke
a pugnacious vapour
a killing fog
a backdraft at a door
we dare not open

and we are, it seems
all of us
climbing sideways

and our ladders
are set on smoke

*as the Canadians were locked in battle in the
regions of Italy leading to Rome, one soldier
said of the desire to move quickly on to Rome,
"Roma puo aspettore" which translates as
"Rome can wait"

Precious Time

Someone on our tour opines

'Why would anyone ever
want to waste an hour
in Rome
by going to the Keats and Shelley Museum
at the base of the Spanish steps?"

he seems to be saying
of poets and their poetry

oh, what a waste of precious time

to think of the young Keats
breathing his last
in the room
at the top of the house
his head on the slip of the pillow
dimpled and cold as marble
fallen there
the deadened wisdom of his statuary brow
with fever chiseled hair

while Fanny in her English grief
can't catch her breath to hear the news
thinks nothing of his words
but rather mourns the stillness
of his heart
she aches and cannot weep
but feels how deep the sorrow goes
when loss is new and real

here busy tourists
laugh and pose and take
the stony stairs
going up and going down
two steps at a time, while careful elders
grip and shuffle
as though they walk on ice

and I am there as well
in the wake of every human shade
I hear the whispering
of truth and beauty
as if the brush that swept
the painted revels almost dancing
on an ancient urn were saying

stranger, pause to listen for
this last unlasting breath
unheard

der Flammenwerfer

"As one great Furnace flam'd, yet from those flames
No light, but rather darkness visible"
Paradise Lost, I, 62-63

like most veterans
of the last great war
he rarely spoke of his time in service
though he fought as a sergeant
in the liberation of Italy, France and Germany
only once did I hear him opine, saying
that the flamethrower
was the most horrifying weapon
known to man

as ancient as Byzantium
belching Greek fire
with Promethean madness

and to think of that liquified flame
coursing through scorching infernos
of blazing air
like a sulphurous serpent
lashing its tongue
licking through ditches
lighting a man
so he'd bloom as though clothed
in incarnadine petals of glory
he'd emit a withering scream
like an ape in a trap

oh, what a devil's adoration are we
who conceive of such things
in our proud imaginings of war

think of soldiers sleeping in trenches
or living in holes
or locked in the metallic guts of armoured machines
caught in a sudden argument of heat and light
come shining through the bones
and shaping the face in a crimson mask of rage

some mother's child, some father's son
become a crimson beast
of blackened fat

a creature in a cold cocoon
a carbon swaddled afterthought
smouldering in a stinking shroud

imago of the ash-winged moth of man
too close the brandished sword of God

Lest We Forget

McCrae's Sorrow:

a contemplation of the poem "In Flanders Fields"

There is a line in Canadian poet Dr. John McRae's oft quoted poem "in Flanders Fields," which has always been problematic for those of us who are committed to peace and understanding in a world gone mad for war. That line: "Take up our quarrel with the foe," is far too easily interpreted out of context as a cry for a continuation of the conflict in the war that was often referred to at the time without a hint of irony as, "the war to end all wars." And the idea that "lest we forget," has as its corollary "never again" is a powerful reminder that warfare is almost always a failure of the human imagination. No one is more opposed to war than a veteran of battle.

As we gather together every November 11th, to honour those who made the major sacrifice in defence of freedom, it might help us all to consider the context of McCrae's intention in the seemingly bellicose line by refreshing our knowledge of the circumstance in which the poem was written.

On May2nd, 1915, McCrae's twenty-two-year-old family friend and sometime companion Lieutenant Alexander Helmer departed from McCrae's company saying, "It has quieted a little. I am going to get some rest." Having said those words, Alexander stepped outside and was immediately blown to bits. McCrae composed the poem "In Flanders Fields" the following day after burying his friend's remains.

It was said of McCrae that he never recovered from the experience and that he took long and solitary rides in the countryside near Ypres on his horse Bonfire. On January 28th, 1918, just two years after composing the poem for which he is famous, at age forty-five, Dr. John McCrae died of pneumonia. It was said of him that he never recovered from the loss of his young friend. He was ever after melancholy, and weary in spirit, suffering perhaps from what was once called 'soldier's heart.'

Who would not feel profound sorrow for the loss he experienced, and who among us would fail to keep faith with those who have died in battle.

Here in translation are the closing lines of Erich Remarque's novel of the same war, All Quiet on the Western Front, on the death of the young protagonist Paul Baumer: "Turning him over one saw that he could not have suffered long; his face had an expression of calm, as though almost glad the end had come."

In my own poem, "Bonfire," I write of McCrae's suffering:

Bonfire

the mind is soaked
in the fallen soldier's sorrowful story
there in memory of weeping ink
only the sound of one sad horse
plodding unheard
under the saddle shadow of a weightless rider
a clip clop gone silent but for the
quietness of imaginary war—endless elsewhere
the absent master sits where he drifts in the light
like smoke above burning
his empty boots facing away from the mane
as though they remained at the foot of his bed
where he dreams on in timeless repose
over unmeasured reams of moonlit darkness
his mount turned to stone
in a vanishing orchard of shade
where he grazes on grass jeweled with dew
see where he sips at the blackening pool
of the soul he has lost
in an autumn of strangers
when evening falls early and soon

and then in the hoar frost of morning
with its white-glazed grasses of dawn
we are late to remember the losses of gloaming
and lest we forget

we lived and were loved
but for the woe of one horse called Bonfire
with his sad fardel of funereal grief

know that he carries us all to the sun
like a lake in a shivering landscape of rain

The Cattling

... poem based on a story told to me by my father-in-law

when Sergeant Morden
saw the need
to move a mob
of dispossessed and displaced
citizens, the diaspora
of the recent war
some of them
sad and ragtag soldiers
disheveled in their tattered
uniforms, wandering
like sheep surrendered
to the shepherd's will
bellwether to a sadness
rung from deep within
the sorrows of the heart
though most
were citizens of an overthrow
old women walking slow
and orphaned lambs
that bleated for
a father's smoky hand
they walked upon a burning map
so mothed in absent towns
and rivers
torn to bridges
so fractured of their purpose
that they lost their meaning
as they spun in ruined stone
like the needle of a compass caught
against the madness of a magnet's dial
like a kite that swirls in heated air
then spears the earth and stabs the ground
and tears the grass
to widow's rags

and there he was
above the bomb-stale streets
the officer in charge
could not get these people on the trucks
he feared they'd riot
out of thirst and hunger
and the common despair
of half-defeated souls

so Sergeant Ernest Otto Morden
sharp of mind
said, "look away …"
and then
he cocked his gun
and said
"Get on the trucks or else
 I'll kill you
 where you stand!"

and so instructed
they obeyed

and this – the cattling
after the war had ceased
and the peace
been signed

—in desperate times
 you do what you must do—

Song of the Lord

a poem composed on the 75th anniversary of the dropping
of the bomb of Hiroshima

"Batter my heart three person God"
*   from "Holy Sonnet" by John Donne*

a stone, a club, a sharpened stick
and anger in the ape
all human wraths become the rage of Caine
the feathered nock, the sharpened flint
the fatal shaft
that quivers in the silent heart
that beats its last within a blood-stained breast
much like the reed stem shivering and gone still
to reveal a dying wind
that passes over the blackened pond
where heaven falls in veils of rain
all armies
gathered in the valley of Jezreel
to live the fletcher's dream
the blacksmith rings
a burning hammer
smelting war
Excalibur extends the magical arm
and open palm to close the fist of ancient kings
and there on the white sands
in the Jornadad del Muerto desert of New Mexico
the mind of man
conceived the end of days

when I was a boy in school
I saw a film
that drew an ashy circle
round a city in Japan
where humans crawled
their bodies masked in dust

old Oppenheimer's ghost
walked out in heavy darkness
though the stars shone through his soul
like sparks in smoke
he said "now I am become death
          destroyer of worlds ..."

and books
with smouldering pages
broke the surface
like the voice of cranes
in white regrets upon upsweeping wings

go fold your paper in the rising sun
magnificent children
given to thoughts of peace

Where the Nightfall Fades

over many years
my uncle John
acquired a barn-sale library
buying up
bins of books
humped in drums
like dead birds dying as they flew
those flap winged remainders
of another's life
where knowledgeable ink bled with rain
the end boards stained by henhouse lime
with proof enough of dust
to pluck the pages
pin-feathered with the decorative gray release
of long neglect   that breath
become the last decade
a good ten years of elder health
spent in study
seated in a chair
in the den on the farm
with Webster open on his lap
slow learning
every word from alpha
through omega
from in the beginning to amen

one time
he called me to the door
to tell me
of a synonym for cider
that word being 'mother'

something every rural woman
of a generation knew
to see the cider
clouded
impure and lovely
fermentation
something strained away
or sometimes
left to work

as over time
the light goes dim
and nothing
but the memory of that man
remains

like books upon a shelf
you read in youth
that fond neglect
of years
meanwhile
the evening trees
adjusting to the dusk
illuminate the darkness
where the nightfall fades

Civilian Sappers

my father and his bachelor brother
who came home from the war
to share the farming
of the land
for seventy years
they sat at the same table
three meals a day
a setting I attended
for seventeen years
from birth through leaving
and although
I knew them both well
from breakfast until bedtime
I worked at the barn
and laboured in the fields
and rode between them in the truck
traveling to the mill, to the fairs
to the stockyard sales
I swear I never, not ever
not ever, not once heard them
have a conversation
beyond yup, and nope
and Uncle John would inquire
"Did she make tea?"
of my mother even though
she was there
in her very own pronomial place
a third person on a dud match

and so when
at my aunt's funeral
one of Uncle John's friends
told me a story
concerning a quarrel
between these two men
on the occasion
of blowing a hole in the earth
to bury a sow
a story involving dynamite
and how George argued
"not enough" and John
retorted "too much"
while George buried three wands
packed them in and over
with clay
and John warned
"It'll blow down into
hard ground" but George won the day
and he lit the fuse
with a dry hiss as it raced
for the wand
and it blew a deep hole
which would serve the purpose

and I'm told
it took four dump truck
loads of earth
to fill the crater left
to solve that argument
between these two amateur sappers
squabbling over TNT

but what pleased me most
was the thought of them
talking – my father George
and his brother, John –
on that day before my time

and when my father passed
John was the last to leave the room
lingering there
where it's the silence
that says the most
in the vigilant quiet
between them

Two Brothers at Peace

Ed Morden served in England during the war doing research into jet engines. He and his brother Ernie met on the ship being sent overseas. When Ed saw Ernie on board, he was startled by his brother's presence there as he said, "Kern, what are you doing here?" Forty years after the war I joined them at Waterford Ponds where we spent the afternoon at peace, casting for fish in the filthy waters of the man-made lakes near my home.

I went fishing
in Waterford ponds
with the Morden brothers
Ed and Ernie
laconic old fellows slogging
the reedy swale
down to the brown-skinned
water, threading night crawlers
on fine hooks and then
casting at heaven
with the doomed reflection
of daylight and poplars
suffused by
rippling circles gone still
lead weight dropping through shallows
to plunk in the mud
on the bed of the pond

what lost blue sky there was
went straying out and off
on that wordless afternoon
toward the soul in silent men
with two hands to the rod
and the feel of the weight as it bends

... in the sixth winter
of the war

that day
a day of snow
thick in the air
like seed kites
of California cottonwood
falling on the city
or the untimely death
of good angels
gone cold in the street
and thick
on the cars in their lots
accreting like ash
from old chimneys
or dust at the mill
and we
were there
at your bedside
in the big cold slab
of bad weather
watching you breathe
in a mask

your heart
gone slow as a stone
on a boat
in a field
heaved by chill in the land—your life
like the hopeloss of those
in the sixth winter
of the last great war
wondering when it might end
like a storm
on the sea in the north

heaving all hands
on its breast in the dark
gone deep
through the waves and
deep through the sky
with no stars
and you were afraid
and coughing for air
on the verge
of an emptying outward
of all that you knew about light

and friends Donald and Roger
came there
from the farm
and they stood
by your bed
in the sanitized misery
of that small room
all three now gone to ghost
like ice from warm glass
the lovely frost flowers of morning
come clear
though they'd formed
in the dark
taken shape in the night

and winter
blends into spring
and the summer-come-autumn
came easing the leaves from their stems
like the delicate winding of watches
that break if you're rough with your hands
and it's been years now
since you were afraid
and catching your breath
in the solstice that came
stealing the stars

each crystal of snow
ones that melt on the tongue
of a child
or the palm of a priest at his prayers
or touching the flow with a fluvial hiss
on the river
unfrozen in motion
and gathering back
what it knows

I Set My Bow in a Cloud

*"I do set my bow in a cloud, and it shall be for a token of a
covenant between me and the earth. And it shall come to pass,
when I bring a cloud over the earth, that the bow shall be seen
in the cloud: And I shall remember my covenant, which is
between me and every living creature of all flesh ..."*
  Genesis 9, xiii-xv

my uncle was a signalman
an expert on the art
of semaphore
I've seen his book of flags
the complicated code
of ship to ship or
ship to shore
stand upon the deck of war
at sea
to have his say
or read the meaning
of the sisterhood
as to the whereabouts
of peril on the waves
the wolf-packed waters
of a shark-infested coast
concealed below the plimsol line
what is the lobo's
word for moon
the light that lay its silks
upon the surface of a swell
like frost on new-ploughed land

this amber covenant
between the darkness
and the night within
the mind of man

how deep the drowning goes
go ask the fish
that's washed ashore
the sailor sunk in dreams
too deep to breathe
he who takes a water breath
like rainbows after rain
might find
the golden moment
at the end of alchemy
like waking from a troubled sleep at dawn

this death he found
with swallow-tail pennons
held well in hand
he clutched at meaning
much like smoke in wind
his final grip below the sheets

A Word
that Only You Can Hear

we are here in the midst
of a perfect storm of stupid
when angry hands
decapitate a brainless bronze
and then
with revolutionary zeal
opinion pikes the past
and sets it
at a wall of living screams
that worm the air with rage

imagine there
the marble brows of Rome
that thoughtless stone
become pontificate of present griefs

or there the old American gentlemen generals
of the civil war that topple
from atop a broken horse
a guano-stained reminder of the pigeons in the park

go dream an empty saddle
go dream a granite beard
combed raw beneath the cannonade
of grappling hands

electric dithyrambs of folly rise with
ill-informed opining
like the weather in a watered wind
that rants against a crag of clay
and eats the absent hill

the empty plinth cries out
as marble spirits will
when acid in the ink
bites through the holy page
and ancient voices burn in books ablaze

the Nazis fires climb, so too
the southern crosses on the lawns of night
while children in devotion
stand and grin
and flicker with an atavistic glee
in Munich and in Birmingham
their faces glowing
from a darkness lit within

poor poets of Etruscan nights
grow quiet
as they vanish
in the bird-scratched
sands of time

tomorrow in the forge
Hephaestus shapes a sword
that looks like me

my tongue a sharpened silence
a quiet flame tipped by a single perilous word
a word that only you can hear

Bird Songs of Tribute: I Remember...

An essay on
Do Songbirds Know Where They're Singing
by Miguel Ángel Olivé Iglesias

War strips the world down to its barest truths—fear, love, loss, and the search for meaning in chaos. For the Canadian soldiers who braved the battlefields of the Second World War, poetry became a vessel to carry their voices across time. Collections such as Rhyme & Reason, published during wartime in "The Maple Leaf" newspaper, and poems preserved in the "Canadian Letters and Images Project," illuminate the emotional landscape of those who served.

Every book carries in its bosom—a word so aptly meaning "source of thoughts and emotions"—the experience, feelings, anecdotes and creative touch of the author. Do Songbirds Know Where They're Singing, by Canada's Poet Laureate John B. Lee, a 2025 Wet Ink Books fresh publication, is filled from cover to cover with a deep, strong, affecting, reverential aura only a few chosen can condense so intensely and pass on to the reader so effectively despite years elapsed. John B. Lee is one such poet. This is a book of poems memorialising the sequels of a war that devastated the human race and stole the lives of numberless soldiers, Canadians included.

Lee's intent is clear: a collection of homage to people he knew (his father-in-law, his Uncle) and closely related to, which adds a personal urge that will appeal to many, and to people, mostly and sadly young boys, who fought in the war and lost their lives. The poet's sensitivity was aroused instantly by the atmosphere surrounding the gravesite he visited. Not only was he moved by the echoing solemnity of the place; he caught as well the symbolic significance of the birds' singing, a detail that did not escape his attention:

"I wondered as I stood by the grave markers of the
fallen Canadians, many as young as 17, 18, and 19, as
I stood in the sound of birds singing, I thought of this
title for a series I hoped to write..."

But there is more in this book of remembrance and honouring.
Respect and a sense of loss envelop the poet. His words, "... to the
young who lost their lives in their late teens and early twenties, a
time when I was in high school, and in early years of university, and I
felt the loss deeply," made me recall José Martí, the Cuban patriot
and Apostle (whom Lee studied and translated), who felt he owed a
sacred debt to his land that he needed to settle as he was abroad in
exile while our 19th-Century War of Independence was being fought
on the island.

Loss is felt both collectively and personally as Lee has family
bonds with those who fought in the war, and he connects on a
spiritual level with the souls of those buried in the cemetery. This
is how he talks about the impact of the visit in his words to the poet
Ola Nowosad:

"I thought the word "loss" as in loss of life, loss of
youth, loss of innocence, loss of peaceful dreaming,
even upon returning home, the cocoon of silence
woven around the horrors of war, the memories
buried so deep in the mind that the psyche could not
handle remembering..."

We need to remember. We need to keep those memories alive
in us and for future generations. Thus, in Lee we have a sentient
poet, a man of honour, a human being shaken by events past his
time, capable of critically construing a dark reality and the bottomless
irrationality of war and death of innocent souls. He explicitly speaks
of armed conflicts as "War is always a failure of the human
imagination." With these essentials, inspired by the birds' musical
sounds, he erects a written monument to the gone and to a
necessary peace.

Lee adheres to and champions what a Jewish scholar said when asked about the Holocaust ("We dare not think to comprehend it, lest by understanding we come to embrace it. It is a sin to even attempt to understand it") and Lee "decrees" what life must be about when he stated in his closing words to Ola, "You must carry a light where you go."

With these conceptions in mind, the poet presents a book of tribute, loss, reverence, sadness, bereavement, and succeeds in getting off his chest the heaviness and anguish of those horrible moments. The poet is putting forward with resolution one of Canada's well-known mottos, "I remember." He remembers, and in remembering he shares his views with the readers so we, too, remember.

While grief defines the emotional core of Lee's poems, another powerful current runs beneath: patriotism. The poet suffers not as an abstract thinker or reader of what happened, but as a being whose acute perceptions allow him to feel and picture death as he treads the fields once reeking of blood, and his country pulses in each tomb.

The book is divided in two segments. The first one includes an introductory poem, a preface-note by Lee and seventeen poems; the second part, entitled Lest We Forget, contains an introduction by the poet and eight poems.

The first poem, "The Songbirds of Auschwitz," begins with the spark that led to the book:

> "what are they singing
> the songbirds of Auschwitz
> and what of the bees
> in the roses of ash
> beneath a blue sky
> which is cloudless and grey..."

The writer starts with rhetorical questions whose pattern he repeats in the second stanza, "what are they singing... and what of the bees..." and "what of the night..." Repetition as an expressive means helps reinforce the message intended by the poet and adds rhythm to it. We cannot forget he is referring to sounds, the singing of birds, the humming of bees. Repetition is a device to reflect the state of mind of a speaker/writer under marked emotion. Stylistically speaking, it aims at logical emphasis, an emphasis necessary to guide the reader's attention towards what a poet wishes to convey and accentuate.

The fact that Lee specifically refers to birds in Auschwitz confers the poem with an atmosphere of contrasts between day and night, between brilliance/light and darkness/blackness of the tragedies still pervading the place.

If we seek answers for the rhetorical questions, we will find them in the poem that entitles the book, "Do the Songbirds Know Where They're Singing." There is no question mark. It is my belief it was the poet's purpose: no need to add the mark as we know what he means and we know what the birds are singing to:

> "... while the songbirds
> sing in glorious celebration
> of the life within
> the fullthroated arias
> of May... /
> ... they seem to be praying
> in song..."
> But, the poet wonders and says,
> "... and do they know anything
> of the sheltered sorrows
> of the war dead... /
> ... of their lost youth
> where they remain
> as reverential dreamers do
> under the stylized stones
> that bear their stolen names..."

Lee wants the reader to breathe in the "full-throated arias / of May" yet he wants us to know—to NOT forget where the birds are singing, that is, "the sheltered sorrows / of the war dead / sleeping there... of their lost youth." Once more and along the pages, the poet describes, reminisces, persists, insists, emphasises the enormous ugliness of the war and the huge toll taken. Read how he ends the piece:

"... that we might know nothing
of the loss
not by a strange indifference
but rather
by an innocent gathering up
of each life unlived
with a given gift
of sixty candles more
for each
and a breath of wishes
to bend each flame within the breast
that's been stilled by the horrors of war"

"Bury them Deep" breaks our hearts as readers. It is so justifiably naturalistic, because it gives us cruelty and indolence, abuse and depravation, soullessness, hatred and scorn. The poem opens this way:

"... bury them deep
for the dogs are hungry
and this then
is the ravenous
appetite of the dogs of war
that these dead boys
should be a meal
to the meaning of moonlight..."
and closes this way,
"... these shallow dogs
that fan the scree
to rattle up
a lifeless hand
these sextants of the dead
make salutations
like a shaken glove
to give a second life its last farewell..."

These are two views of the irony of war, of the Grim Reaper's harrowing banquet. The poet's proposal in the two sides of the text drills far into our sentiments.

I said earlier that Lee is not as an abstract thinker or reader of what happened. He is someone whose acute perceptions allow him to feel and picture, crossing a temporal portal. This is noticed in his lines from "Walking the Streets of Florence":

"I tell you reader
I was there
and I felt the quitting
of the quickening wet
like the drying of the fabric
on a laundry line
with blood within my marrow bone
and spittle breath
within these words
like ink that glittered on the pages
of an empty tomb..."

Lee evolves from being a tourist to being an informed witness of what occurred years ago on those same streets he now walks.

If I said that the poet was being openly naturalistic in "Bury Them Deep," read the lines below from "der Flammenwerfer":

"... and to think of that liquified flame
coursing through scorching infernos
of blazing air
like a sulphurous serpent
lashing its tongue
licking through ditches
lighting a man
so he'd bloom as though clothed
in incarnadine petals of glory
he'd emit a withering scream
like an ape in a trap..."

The description makes our hearts cringe and our skins flinch. The images the poet conjures serve as a still kind example of the horrors of the war and the misdeeds of the Germans. However, Lee won't stop at that. He uses irony, poignantly, to criticize the minds of those who wrought havoc,

> "oh, what a devil's adoration are we
> who conceive of such things
> in our proud imaginings of war…"

And again, the hurting poet vividly—oh so vividly—depicts more meanness, more desperation:

> "… some mother's child, some father's son
> become a crimson beast
> of blackened fat
>
> a creature in a cold cocoon
> a carbon swaddled afterthought
> smouldering in a stinking shroud…"

The next section, Lest We Forget, is an ode to the aftermath of loss and the senselessness of fighting wars and taking lives. In his intro words, Lee tells us "warfare is almost always a failure of the human imagination. No one is more opposed to war than a veteran of battle." Those who fought and could be "home free" became awfully aware of what wars do or rather undo and destroy. The suffering of Canadian poet Dr. John McRae is reflected in Lee's own poem "Bonfire":

> "the mind is soaked
> in the fallen soldier's sorrowful story
> there in memory of weeping ink
> only the sound of one sad horse
> plodding unheard
> under the saddle shadow of a weightless rider
> a clip clop gone silent but for the
> quietness of imaginary war—endless elsewhere…"

The poet paints a gloomy scene. He resorts to description, personalisation, onomatopoeia, epithets to render his narrative striking and to the point. Let us not fail in noticing that the stanza ends with an interesting, miserably true remark, "... war—endless elsewhere," that brings to the surface the escalation of conflicts nowadays.

The section's coda poem "I Set My Bow in the Cloud" closes with these lines:

> "... my tongue a sharpened silence
> a quiet flame tipped by a single perilous word
> a word that only you can hear"

Lee's tongue is now in silence but sharpened; in silence but reverencing the gone and singing, like the birds, to bravery and hope.

For today's reader, especially younger generations, Lee's poems create an intimacy with history. Reading them is like holding a soldier's hand on site across decades, hearing a whisper through the debris of war: "We were here. We mattered." Somehow we are transported to a Canadian soldier being cared for by a comrade in the Price of Peace Monument in Ortona, Italy.

This review barely scratches the surface. In remembering the legacy of Canadian WWII soldiers, we also reclaim their heroism and sacrifice. Sometimes lines of poetry can speak louder than history books can. I suggest you read this book ready to tremble and evoke, ready to acknowledge and revere. John B. Lee remembers, so do we.

Thank you, John.

Prof. Miguel Ángel Olivé Iglesias. MSc
Literary Essayist, Poet, Prose Writer, Editor, Translator
Vice-president of the Canada Caribbean Literary Alliance

Hidden Brook Press and Wet Ink Books
by John B. Lee

Do Songbirds Know Where They're Singing
— 978-1-998324-24-8

The Last Stand
— 978-1-998324-14-9

Darling, may I touch your pinkletink
— 978-1-989786-05-5

In the Arc Welder's Blinding Light
— 978-1-989786-74-1

Riddle Me This
— 978-1-989786-47-5

In the Muddy Shoes of Morning
— 978-1-897475-64-5

This is How We See the World
— 978-1-927725-50-4

Island on the Wind-Breathed Edge of the Sea
— 978-1-897475-19-5

These are the words
George Elliott Clarke and John B. Lee
— 978-1-927725-55-9

In This We Hear The Light
with photographer Richard M. Grove
— 978-1-897475-96-6

Editor of:
The Beauty of Being Elsewhere: poems of journey and sojourn
— 978-1-989786-43-7

Window Fishing — 1st, 2nd and 3rd Editions
— 978-1-927725-41-2

About the Author

John B. Lee has published nearly one hundred books, and is the editor of nearly a dozen anthologies. Appointed Poet Laureate of the city of Brantford in perpetuity, he is also Poet Laureate of Norfolk County for life, and Poet Laureate of the Canada Caribbean Literary Alliance. Called "the greatest living poet in English," by George Whipple, he is a recipient of well over one hundred prestigious national and international awards for his writing.

His most recent books include Stronger in Broken Places (Aeolus House, 2024), The Last Stand (Wet Ink Books, 2024) and A Wet Seed Wild in the Hot Blind Earth (Aeolus House, 2025). He is currently working on The Tree of Common Sorrows, a sequel to Do Songbirds Know Where They're Singing.

He lives with his wife Cathy in a lake house overlooking Long Point Bay on Lake Erie in the town of Port Dover.

www.ingramcontent.com/pod-product-compliance
Lightning Source LLC
Chambersburg PA
CBHW020800130626
46554CB00006B/2286